The Outrageous Adventures of Sheldon & Mrs. Levine

A Son's Elusive Search for His Mother's Happiness

by Sam Bobrick and Julie Stein

A SAMUEL FRENCH ACTING EDITION

FOUNDED 1830
NEW YORK HOLLYWOOD LONDON TORONTO
SAMUELFRENCH.COM

Copyright © 1997, 2004, 2009 by Sam Bobrick and Julie Stein

ALL RIGHTS RESERVED

CAUTION: Professionals and amateurs are hereby warned that *THE OUTRAGEOUS ADVENTURES OF SHELDON & MRS. LEVINE* is subject to a Licensing Fee. It is fully protected under the copyright laws of the United States of America, the British Commonwealth, including Canada, and all other countries of the Copyright Union. All rights, including professional, amateur, motion picture, recitation, lecturing, public reading, radio broadcasting, television and the rights of translation into foreign languages are strictly reserved. In its present form the play is dedicated to the reading public only.

The amateur live stage performance rights to *THE OUTRAGEOUS ADVENTURES OF SHELDON & MRS. LEVINE* are controlled exclusively by Samuel French, Inc., and licensing arrangements and performance licenses must be secured well in advance of presentation. PLEASE NOTE that amateur Licensing Fees are set upon application in accordance with your producing circumstances. When applying for a licensing quotation and a performance license please give us the number of performances intended, dates of production, your seating capacity and admission fee. Licensing Fees are payable one week before the opening performance of the play to Samuel French, Inc., at 45 W. 25th Street, New York, NY 10010.

Licensing Fee of the required amount must be paid whether the play is presented for charity or gain and whether or not admission is charged.

Stock licensing fees quoted upon application to Samuel French, Inc.

For all other rights than those stipulated above, apply to: Abrams Artists Agency 275 Seventh Avenue, 26th Floor, New York, NY 10001 Attn: Ron Gwiazda.

Particular emphasis is laid on the question of amateur or professional readings, permission and terms for which must be secured in writing from Samuel French, Inc.

Copying from this book in whole or in part is strictly forbidden by law, and the right of performance is not transferable.

Whenever the play is produced the following notice must appear on all programs, printing and advertising for the play: "Produced by special arrangement with Samuel French, Inc."

Due authorship credit must be given on all programs, printing and advertising for the play.

ISBN 978-0-573-63049-1   Printed in U.S.A.   #21485

No one shall commit or authorize any act or omission by which the copyright of, or the right to copyright, this play may be impaired.

No one shall make any changes in this play for the purpose of production.

Publication of this play does not imply availability for performance. Both amateurs and professionals considering a production are strongly advised in their own interests to apply to Samuel French, Inc., for written permission before starting rehearsals, advertising, or booking a theatre.

No part of this book may be reproduced, stored in a retrieval system, or transmitted in any form, by any means, now known or yet to be invented, including mechanical, electronic, photocopying, recording, videotaping, or otherwise, without the prior written permission of the publisher.

IMPORTANT BILLING AND CREDIT REQUIREMENTS

All producers of *THE OUTRAGEOUS ADVENTURES OF SHELDON & MRS. LEVINE* must give credit to the Authors of the Play in all programs distributed in connection with performances of the Play, and in all instances in which the title of the Play appears for the purposes of advertising, publicizing or otherwise exploiting the Play and/or a production. The name of the Authors *must* appear on a separate line on which no other name appears, immediately following the title and *must* appear in size of type not less than fifty percent of the size of the title type.

THE OUTRAGEOUS ADVENTURES OF SHELDON & MRS. LEVINE played at the Falcon Theatre in Burbank, Californian from October 17 to November 18, 2007. The production was directed by John Bowab, produced by Garry K. Marshall and Kathleen Marshall, with Arnold Margolin as Producing Director and Sherry Santillano as Production Manager. The cast and crew was as follows:

MRS. LEVINE. . . . . Sally Struthers
SHELDON. . . . . Jeff Marlow

Set Design – Keith Mitchell
Costume Design – Denitsa Bliznakova
Lighting Design – Jeremy Pivnick
Sound Design – Robert Arturo Ramirez
Stage Manager/Prop Design – Deirdre Murphy

CHARACTERS

MRS. LEVINE – a woman in her mid-fifties
SHELDON – her thirty-one year-old son

PRODUCTION NOTE

The play is an exchange of letters between two characters who use journals to mime the writing of their letters, when they are actually reading their lines. Mrs. Levine has three journals for Act I and one journal for Act II. Sheldon has one journal for the entire play. Only Sheldon's final speech in Act I, Scene 2, Mrs. Levine's final speech in Act I, Scene 3 and the last four pages of Act II require memorization.

A NOTE FROM THE PLAYWRIGHTS

We felt the need to publish a revised version of the play after our fall 2007 production at Garry Marshall's Falcon Theatre in Burbank, California. Under the direction of the incredibly talented John Bowab and with amazing performances from our cast, Sally Struthers and Jeff Marlow, we made significant cuts and changes which we felt would benefit all future productions.

–Sam Bobrick and Julie Stein
2009

ACT I

Scene One

*(**TIME:** The present)*

*(**THE SET:** The set is divided into two areas.)*

*(Stage right is **MRS. LEVINE**'s kitchen area. This can be either a simple set consisting of a kitchen table and two chairs facing the audience with a refrigerator behind them against the upstage right wall, or a more realistic kitchen with an island counter with two stools facing the audience and behind them against the upstage right wall, a refrigerator and a non-functioning stove and sink.)*

(Stage left is a limbo set used by both characters on their journeys of self-discovery. This set consists of three raised platforms, small, medium and large, stacked on one another with enough playing space for the actors to sit or walk around on. Offstage, at upstage left, are stairs that access the top platform. A safety railing runs along the backside, parallel to the upstage left wall. A small cube is placed on the top platform for use as an additional seat. To add visual depth to our characters respective journeys, images can be projected on the cyc, such as a Tibetan mountain monastery, oncoming headlights, prison bars, etc. Unless otherwise noted, the blocking will be left to the interpretation of the Director.)

*(**MRS. DORIS LEVINE**, a woman in her mid-fifties, dressed in a housecoat and slippers, ENTERS from stage right. She carries a handful of junk mail and crosses to the island counter where she goes through the mail.)*

MRS. LEVINE. Save the whales, Save the trees, Save the planet...

(discarding them in a nearby trash can)

Save the postage.

(sits down on one of the stools, picks up her journal and pen and begins to mime writing)

To Mr. Sheldon Levine, in care of the California Missing Persons Bureau. Dear Sheldon. Two weeks have gone by since you moved to California and I haven't heard from you. How long are you going to keep up this silent treatment? I'm your mother. It's your job as my son not to aggravate me. Please let me know if you're dead or alive. Every day I don't hear from you is another day off my life. If you're trying to kill me, it's working. Love, you mother, who's already starting to forget what you look like.

SHELDON. *(O.S.)* Forget what I look like!

(Wearing a small bandage on his head and carrying his journal, **SHELDON** *ENTERS upstage left, sits on the cube and angrily begins writing.)*

Mrs. Doris Levine, 2241 Marshall Avenue, Apartment number 301, New Rochelle, New York, 10108. Dear Mother. Please don't write to me anymore in care of the Missing Persons Bureau. There was a mix up in their search and a bunch of cops knocked my door down and beat the crap out of me. Haven't you done enough damage? I'm thirty-one years old and you're sucking the life out of me. Your ex-son Sheldon. P.S. I will never forgive you for giving my wife Brenda ten thousand dollars to leave me.

(He EXITS upstage left.)

MRS. LEVINE. Mr. Sheldon Levine, in care of the California Missing Persons Bureau. Dear Sheldon. How long are you going to blame me for the breakup of your marriage? I was only trying to protect you. You were too naïve to see that obnoxious ex-wife of yours hated me from the day I moved into the apartment next to you. Love mother. P.S. I called Dr. Laura on her radio show. Believe it or not, she cried more than I did. P.S. P.S. I think I had a small stroke yesterday.

SHELDON. *(ENTERS upstage left wearing a larger bandage on his head)* Dear Mother. I'm tired of the police beating me up every time you try to contact me. If you must write, send it to P.O. Box twenty-six eighty-seven, Los Angeles, California. You can't imagine the pain I'm in thanks to you. Now I know why Dad died so young. He wanted to. P.S. I'm sick of all those talk show quacks you listen to, so tell Dr. Laura to piss off.

MRS. LEVINE. Sheldon, my darling son, my life and now Post Office Box twenty-six eighty-seven. I only hope and pray that one day you will have children who will break your heart as you've broken mine. Since you moved away I can't eat, I can't sleep, I can't get out of bed.

(bites into a Pastry)

This afternoon, while having lunch at Bagel Heaven I bumped into Dr. Melnick. He said I looked like hell. I was so upset I could hardly finish the fries that came with my pastrami sandwich. By the way, I heard that your prima donna ex-wife used the money I gave her to get a nose job and now she wants to be a model. I always knew she was delusional. P. S. I worry about your penmanship. The way you slash your t's and draw snakes and spiders all over your letters makes me think you have a very dark side. For your sake, I hope I'm wrong.

SHELDON. Dear Mother. When I pick up your letters my hands shake. I start to sweat and feel nauseous. You get me so upset I can't even concentrate on my poetry which I abandoned years ago because you insisted that I become an accountant.

MRS. LEVINE. Dear Sheldon. About your poetry. Believe me when I tell you, you're not gifted in that area and who knows you better than me? Come home and get back into accounting where you belong, and so I can hold my head up high when people ask me what my son does. Love, your Mother, who risked her life bringing you into this world and don't you forget it.

SHELDON. Dear Mother. ROSES ARE RED, VIOLETS ARE BLUE. I GET SICK, JUST THINKING OF YOU. Love, Sheldon.

MRS. LEVINE. Dear Sheldon. I read your poem to all the girls at my bridge club. Three of them liked it and the other twenty-four said you should take Prozac. And while I'm on the subject of serious illnesses, Doctor Melnick took X-rays and he doesn't like what he sees. Love, your ailing Mother, who when she's not thinking of you, is shopping for a head stone.

(**MRS. LEVINE** *coughs a little, clutches her heart.*)

SHELDON. Dear Mother. I called Doctor Melnick and he said you're as healthy as a horse. Don't ever try to put me on a guilt trip again because I'm not buying it. How many sons besides me, took their mother to the prom? Because of you, I have no confidence, no self esteem and above all, no wife. I detest you. Sheldon.

(*He EXITS upstage left to remove head bandage.*)

MRS. LEVINE. Dear Sheldon. Happy Birthday my ray of sunshine. I hope you like the card I sent.

SHELDON. (*ENTERS upstage left carrying an enormous card and reads.*) BIRTHDAY GREETINGS FOR MY BIRTHDAY BOY. I HOPE THIS DAY BRINGS YOU LOTS OF JOY. MAY ALL YOUR DREAMS IN LIFE COME TRUE. EXCEPT THE ONES ABOUT BRENDA COMING BACK TO YOU. Love, Mother.

(*He puts card aside.*)

MRS. LEVINE. I went in and out of stationary stores all day until I found the perfect one. Maybe that's how I caught the flu and am now sick as a dog.

(*coughs*)

MRS. LEVINE. *(cont.)* Doctor Shuckmeyer, who I now go to instead of that big mouth Melnick, says I must move to a warmer climate. I hope you have an extra bedroom.

SHELDON. Forget it. Don't even think about coming out here because you'll never find me.

MRS. LEVINE. Dear Sheldon. You don't own Los Angeles. If I want to come, I'll come. I don't need your address. If I have to go house to house, I'll find you. There is nothing stronger than a mother's love, no matter how unjustly her only son treats her. As always, your tormented mother.

SHELDON. Oh, please! Don't talk to me about torment. I saw Brenda's picture on the cover of six fashion magazines this month. She's even more beautiful with her new nose. I'll never stop loving her or hating you. I hate you, I hate you, I hate you. Love, Sheldon.

MRS. LEVINE. *(fed up)* Dear Sheldon. Stop already with the Brenda thing. I promise, one day you'll thank me for getting rid of her. I can honestly tell from your letters how much healthier you are without that viper in your life. Now, even though it's cold and icy and I have bad knees, I think after I finish watching Divorce Court, People's Court and Judge Judy, I'll go out and check on the air fares to California. Please don't blame yourself if I get hit by a bus.

SHELDON. Dear Mother. If indeed I am sounding healthier it's because I'm three thousand miles away from you. Come to California if you want, but I won't be here. I'm moving again and don't bother trying to find me because this time you never will. So long forever. Sheldon.

MRS. LEVINE. Mr. Sheldon Levine. 151 Main Street. Bismarck, North Dakota. Dear Sheldon. You can run, but you can't hide. Love, your ever-present Mother.

SHELDON. *(bewildered)* Mother! I can't believe it. How did you find me? I must know! Sheldon.

MRS. LEVINE. I owe it all to a class I'm taking at the senior center. "Clairvoyance for Beginners." We're learning to get in touch with all the untapped powers each of us possess. I can see your every move.

(She closes her eyes, rubs her temples as if in a trance. **SHELDON** *bites his fingernails.)*

Quit biting your fingernails...

*(***SHELDON*** looks at her frightened, and stops.)*

And if I've told you once, I've told you a thousand times, *lift* the toilet seat when you pee. Love, your newly remodeled mother.

SHELDON. Dear Mother. You're giving me the creeps. I'm moving again and this time I'm changing my name too. You'll never find me. Never, never, N-E-V-E-R. Sheldon for now, but not for long.

MRS. LEVINE. To Miss Scarlett O'Hara. 4675 Magnolia Avenue. Atlanta, Georgia. Dear Scarlett, formerly Sheldon. Nice try but give up. I can see your every move. You'll never be able to escape me again. Besides visions of you, I also get HBO and the Playboy channel. Oh, Sheldon, I'm so excited about the opening of my mystical doors. Who knows where they might lead me? Love, your supernaturally enhanced mother.

SHELDON. Dear Mother. I feel so naked, so violated. Are you possessed? Am I possessed? Is this all a bad dream? Let go! Get out of my life! I beg you! Your pushing me over the edge. I'm afraid of what I might do. Yours truly, Mad Dog Levine.

(He snarls like a rabid dog. Beat.)

Dear Mother. It was a welcomed relief not hearing from you this week. I've almost gotten control of myself. I hardly scream in public anymore.

(another beat)

Mother! I haven't heard from you in three weeks. And while I've enjoyed every minute, I can't help thinking you're up to something. Could I be wrong?

(Another beat. Whinny)

SHELDON. *(cont.)* Mom. You're killing me. It's been four and a half weeks and I still haven't heard from you. Is something the matter? I'm a little concerned. Your son…

MRS. LEVINE. *(very peacefully)* Sheldon. I've been thinking it over. You're right. You need your freedom, your space to grow. I've learned through my recent encounter with the metaphysical world that we must each tend our own celestial garden so that our souls can blossom and flourish. Therefore, I'm cutting you loose.

SHELDON. What do you mean you're cutting me loose? And what's with this garden bullshit? You just look at a plant and it dies. You'd better not be screwing with my head again. One thing I know for sure, Doris Levine doesn't let go so easily. Something doesn't sound right. What's going on?

MRS. LEVINE. Dear Sheldon. You'll never believe it. I'm getting married…to my clairvoyance teacher. His name is Akbar and he's from India. He taught me to meditate and Sheldon, for the first time I've actually been able to quiet my mind. Sometimes the silence gives me a migraine. Oh, Sheldon, there is so much more to life than I ever imagined. I have learned to achieve serenity and happiness by dancing around a flower, chanting at the airport and avoiding fried foods. Well, gotta go put on a bed sheet. The gang's waiting for me. Love, your karmically upgraded mother.

(She EXITS stage right chanting.)

Ohmmmm! Ohmmmm! Ohmmmm!

SHELDON. *(fear stricken)* Dear Mom. Something's rotten in New Rochelle. Why are you talking like a nut? Serenity? Happiness? I didn't even know you knew those words. And what's with this marriage business? You already had a husband. Why would God want to punish another one? This is definitely a step backwards for our relationship. I'm worried so I'm coming home. Don't do anything without me. If this is my fault

I'm really sorry. I know I've been less than the perfect son, but it's never too late to make amends. I'll do all the things you wanted me to do when I was a kid. I'll throw out the garbage, I'll pick up my dirty socks and I promise to stop eating Cheese Doodles in the living room. I'm coming home, Mom! I'm coming home.

(He crosses backstage and RE-ENTERS stage right.)

Mom? It's me! Your loving son, Sheldon. Where are you?

(He looks under the counter. Sing-Song.)

Come out, come out, wherever you are.

(Notices a letter on the counter. He picks it up and reads.)

MRS. LEVINE. *(PRE-RECORDED V.O.)* Dear Sheldon. If I was meant to be here, I would be. But I'm not, so I wasn't. Don't wait up for me. I may not be back for years. Love, your remarkably metamorphosized mother, who is now embarking on the first real adventure of her life.

*(**SHELDON** lowers the letter with a stricken look on his face.)*

SHELDON. Oh my God, at the age of thirty-one, I'm an abandoned child.

(fade to black)

Scene Two

(In the background we hear Eastern Indian music. Lights up as **MRS. LEVINE** *appears on the highest platform upstage left. She now wears a sari and has a small shoulder pouch to carry her journal and pen. She sits on the cube, takes out her journal and pen and begins writing.)*

MRS. LEVINE. Mr. Sheldon Levine, 2241 Marshall Avenue, New Rochelle, New York. Dear Sheldon. My new husband, Akbar, and I are now honeymooning in a Tibetan monastery where I am cooking for six hundred monks. The sacrifice and hard work which I am experiencing seems to bring a certain tranquility to me that was definitely missing before. I am now able to understand what is important in life and what is not. Love and kindness are important. A cheesecake is not. It's a whole new concept, but I think I'm getting it. Please write me in care of General Delivery, Tibet. Love, Mother Bakahuta.

SHELDON. Dear Mother Bakahuta-my-ass. You are Doris *Levine* and that's all you'll ever be. Unless this monastery has a gift shop I don't believe a word you're telling me. You, the queen of take-out food, cooking for all those Monks, that's a laugh. And this tranquility crap. The only time you're content is when you make me miserable. And why did you get rid of all the furniture? There's no bed, there's no sofa, the only place I can sleep is in the bathtub and the stupid faucet leaks. I'm very confused by all this, not to mention stiff and damp. You have a lot of explaining to do, Doris *Levine*. Regards, Sheldon. P.S. I'm starting to get angry again.

MRS. LEVINE. My darling Sheldon. Akbar has taught me that anger is a completely useless emotion. It only clouds ones judgment and wears out your pancreas. As for the furniture, Akbar has taught me that ones journey through life must be made as simply and unencumbered as possible. Therefore, I donated everything to the Salvation Army, except of course your father's ashes. Those I put in cold storage with my fur coats.

(Sound: Gong)

MRS. LEVINE. *(cont.)* Well, gotta run. It's lunch time and I need to boil twelve hundred pounds of rice.

(Sound: Gong)

(annoyed)

I'm coming! I'm coming!

(She EXITS upstage left.)

SHELDON. Dear Mother. It sounds like you bought yourself a husband and he bought himself a green card. Guys like this prey on women like you constantly. They're cunning and shifty and only care about themselves. So even though you have a lot in common, my advice is to kiss off this jerk right now and catch the next plane back here. If Dad knew how you're carrying on he'd turn over in his urn.

*(**MRS. LEVINE** ENTERS upstage left.)*

MRS. LEVINE. Dear Sheldon. Funny you should mention your dead father. Just last night he came to me in a dream and told me he was very proud of my spiritual growth and approved of my marriage to Akbar. He seemed happier than he's been in years. The man finally found something that agrees with him. Death!

SHELDON. *(pacing, as he writes in his journal)* Mother. I'm so unhappy I don't know why I came back home. I'm lonely and artistically stifled. I've been working on my poetry and have spent the past three days trying to find a word that rhymes with sigmoidoscopy. It's so hard to be creative and suicidal at the same time.

MRS. LEVINE. Dearest Sheldon. Akbar said a lonely soul is a wasted soul and thinks you need a pet. How about a gold fish? They're loyal and devoted and best of all, when they die you can just flush them down the toilet. Love, Mother B.

SHELDON. Dear Mom. I took Akbar's advice and bought a parrot. His name is Roberto.

(He pulls out a prop parrot from below the counter and slams it down.)

SHELDON. *(cont.)* He only speaks Spanish, so I never know what the hell he's saying. The similarities between you and Roberto are amazing. You both have beady eyes and a spastic colon. Still depressed as ever, Sheldon.

MRS. LEVINE. Dear Sheldon. I continue to blossom and learn from Akbar. This is an incredible experience and a gift from the universe. The only problem is the monks use so much incense sometimes this place smells like a hooker on a hot bus. I'm sorry happiness is still eluding you. Akbar said you should get a hobby. He suggested sky diving.

SHELDON. Dear Mom. Akbar's an asshole. Last week I joined your bridge club hoping that all those women bitching and moaning would remind me of happier times. I was wrong. I lost five dollars and thirty cents. I think Mrs. Minkus cheats. The back of her cards never match the rest of the deck. But what really disturbed me was that every time I mentioned Akbar's name, Mrs. Krinski would throw herself on the floor and start kicking and screaming. What's her problem?

MRS. LEVINE. Dear Sheldon. Pay no attention to Mrs. Krinski. She's just upset that I have a man and she doesn't. There is no need to fear Akbar. He's a very gentle and loving soul. When we take long walks in the wilderness, ferocious lions and tigers come up and nuzzle him for affection. A marvelous show of comradery between man and beast. Sometimes my sweet Akbar will spend hours kissing and hugging them. I, on the other hand, climb up a tree faster than a monkey in heat.

SHELDON. Dear Mother. I was thrown out of your stupid bridge club. I followed your advice and left the toilet seat up and Mrs. Minkus almost drowned. I am crippled by anxiety attacks and rejection. Sheldon.

MRS. LEVINE. Dear Sheldon. Akbar feels all your bitching and moaning is just another sign of your immaturity and he's having second thoughts about adopting you. Snap out of it and stop feeling sorry for yourself. Life is not as shitty as you want it to be. I saw that written on the wall in the monk's bathroom.

SHELDON. *(upset)* Dear Mother. When I woke up this morning my parrot, Roberto, was gone. I feel more abandoned than ever. First Brenda, then you and now the goddamn parrot. What do I do?

MRS. LEVINE. Dear Sheldon. Sorry about your bird. Akbar recalled an old adage.

(in an Eastern-Indian accent)

"If you love something, let it go. If it doesn't come back, it's just as well. It would probably crap on the carpet anyway."

SHELDON. Dear Mother. I'm starting to do crazy things and I don't know why. Yesterday I went into a mini-mart and shoplifted a banana. I don't even like bananas.

MRS. LEVINE. Akbar said the next time you're in one of those stores, buy a lottery ticket. He feels very strongly about the numbers 3-7-16-29-42 and 43.

SHELDON. Akbar is a fraud. He didn't pick one lottery number right. I'm more suspicious of him than ever.

MRS. LEVINE. Akbar gave you the wrong lottery numbers on purpose. He said it was time you learned to deal with disappointment like a grown up.

SHELDON. I did something crazy again. I held up a guy on the street with just the banana. I got his wallet, his pants and one shoe. What is it with me and this banana?

MRS. LEVINE. It's very simple. It's your diet. You're not getting enough fiber. Oh, Sheldon, being at one with the universe is what life is all about. It's just like Nietzsche said, or maybe it was Regis Philbin: "It's not what you take from life that really matters, it's what you give." I never used to believe that crap before, but now I've really come around. P.S. Akbar has promised to teach me to make contact with inanimate objects. It should be easy. I was married to one for almost thirty years. Only kidding. Just a little monastery humor.

SHELDON. Dear Mother. I was standing in front of the Plaza Hotel and saw Brenda getting into a limo. She was with Puff Daddy and looked gorgeous. I was smelly and dirty and needed a shave. As she was pulling away she rolled down her window and tossed me a buck. Oh, Mom, I still love her.

MRS. LEVINE. Dear Sheldon. I beg you, forget Brenda. Use the buck to buy another lottery ticket. If you win you can get any woman you want. Tomorrow Akbar and I are going on an astral journey.

SHELDON. *(turning to her)* A what?

MRS. LEVINE. *(turning to him)* An astral journey! To explore the spiritual treasures of infinity. We got a wonderful package. Four centuries in four days.

SHELDON. Dear Mom. I called every travel agent in the city and there is no such thing as an astral journey. I think this is just another way of your avoiding reality.

MRS. LEVINE. Akbar explained that reality is an over-rated concept that has been given far too much importance. If the Wright Brothers allowed themselves to be hampered by reality, we never would have the airplane. The same goes for Thomas Edison and the light bulb and what about that incredible guy who invented Viagra. As Akbar has said time and time again…

(in an Eastern-Indian accent)

"If we are to grow, we must never let reality get in the way of our dreams."

SHELDON. Dear Mother. It's obvious that Akbar is the cause of all our current problems. I went to see a witch doctor who I looked up in the yellow pages. He said he would be able to solve everything for fifty bucks. I gave it to him. What the hell.

MRS. LEVINE. Dear Sheldon, you little bastard. Yesterday Akbar and I went for our usual walk in the wilderness and he was eaten by his favorite tiger. The same one who use to lick his face, swallowed him in one gulp.

SHELDON. Whoa! A tiger! Imagine that. And for just fifty bucks. What a good investment.

MRS. LEVINE. I'm really mad, Sheldon. Just because I ruined your marriage doesn't mean you had to ruin mine. Lucky for you, Akbar taught me that

(in Eastern Indian accent)

"Death, as well as life, is just one of the dimensions we must pass through to reach our final Utopia."

(in her normal voice)

Anyway, since you're all I have left, I have no alternative but to release my sorrow to the cosmos and come home. See you soon. Love, the widow Bakahuta. P.S. It would be very thoughtful of you to pick up a couple cans of cream soda for me. That's the only thing I really missed besides soft toilet paper.

(She EXITS upstage left.)

SHELDON. *(Elated. To Audience. Memorized)* She's coming home! Mom is coming home! Oh, boy! Everything is going to be so wonderful now...You would think... wouldn't you? I would. Why shouldn't I? She's a changed woman. She's wise and worldly and...and... and...Oh, my God. I'm still...Sheldon.

(He takes a pen and piece of paper and begins writing.)

Dear Mother. I'm finally becoming aware of your astounding growth and I'm frightened. You seem to have discovered the harmonious rhythm of the universe while I remain the same stagnant piece of crap I've always been. Therefore, I too must make a soul enlightening journey to ignite my spirit and reach my true potential. Beneath my venomous anger, there must be a kinder, gentler Sheldon. I must seek that Sheldon out and tell him to get his shit together. I love you, mother, but unless I am satisfied with who I am, how can I expect you to be? Although I don't have any idea what my final destination will be, the idea of brotherly love sticks in my mind, so for now I'm heading to Philadelphia. You can write me there in care of General Delivery. Love, Sheldon.

(Places his letter on the counter. He addresses the audience. Memorized)

SHELDON. *(cont.)* Who'd ever think that a day would come when a child would want to be exactly like his parent? Jeez. Life is full of surprises.

(He EXITS stage right.)

(blackout)

Scene Three

(Lights up on stage right.)

MRS. LEVINE. *(O.S.)* Sheldon? Sheldon?

*(*MRS. LEVINE ENTERS *stage right dressed in black. She notices Sheldon's letter on the counter, picks it up looks at it briefly, puts it down and begins writing. She is annoyed.)*

Dear Sheldon. For someone who bellyached about how much he needed me, I can't tell you how disappointed I was not to find you home. Once again I'm reminded how difficult it is to be your mother.

(Lights up Stage left as **SHELDON** ENTERS *upstage left on the top platform, wearing a light jacket and carrying a small backpack. He sits and begins writing.)*

(Sound: Truck roaring by)

SHELDON. Dear Mom. I've been hitchhiking for a week and a half now, and although it's going quite slowly I've really made some profound observations. People are not as friendly as I thought they would be. So far I've been mugged four times and shot at twice. But I'm hoping things will get a little better once I get out of Newark. Oh, mother, for the first time in my life I feel as if there's genuine hope for me. Love, Sheldon.

MRS. LEVINE. Dear Sheldon. It's nice to be home but oh, I miss Akbar deeply. There's an emptiness inside me that I'm not sure will ever be filled again. Not even by meditating or getting a good frisking at the airport. Fortunately, the wisdom I've gathered over these past few months kicked in and I stopped being angry with you after the second week. It's amazing how serenity can come and go like a head cold.

SHELDON. Dear Mother. I had to walk most of the way to Philadelphia, but it was worth it just to see the Liberty Bell. While to some, the crack in it stands as a symbol of freedom, I was only reminded that shoddy goods were made in those days too. As I left Independence Hall, I was nearly run over by a pick up truck. The truck had a bumper sticker that said "Logan, West Virginia – You'll Find It Here." I felt it was another sign so I'm planning to hop a freight and head there. Boy, this is exciting.

MRS. LEVINE. General Delivery. Logan, West Virginia. Dear Sheldon. I didn't realize how much I missed TV. Especially all my wonderful talk shows. In the past I always found watching people who were more miserable and desperate than I was totally uplifting. Although the new me can no longer relate to those negative feelings, I still find watching those shows an absolute joy.

SHELDON. Dear Mother. I'm not in West Virginia yet. I hopped a freight train but after four days of not moving I realized it was an abandoned car. I'll keep trying.

MRS. LEVINE. Dear Sheldon. I went to play bridge with the girls. All they did was bitch, bitch, bitch. Normally, I would have enjoyed it, but since my cosmic expansion I realize they're much too shallow to appreciate the flowering of my soul. So, as my beloved Akbar used to say...

(in Eastern-Indian accent)

"Fuck them all."

(normal voice)

Love Mother.

SHELDON. Dear Mother. I'm still not in West Virginia yet. The train hit a cow and I fell off. I then experienced one of the most awe inspiring moments in my life. Although the cow was thrown several hundred feet in the air and landed on her head, with great determination she got up, shrugged her shoulders and continued walking down the road triumphantly. I was unable to contain myself because this cow, with all her courage and strength, reminded me of you – and I mean that in a good way. I began applauding and shouting, "You Go Girl! You Go Girl!" Unfortunately when the cow turned her head to see what all the yelling was about, she was hit by a speeding truck and this time flattened for good. I am sure that in my travels I will meet someone who will be able to make sense of this tragedy. Love, Sheldon.

MRS. LEVINE. Last night I had dinner with Malcolm Bass, the man you held up with the banana. He was thrilled to get his wallet, shoe and pants back. Malcolm's a dance instructor, which I'm sure has helped preserve his youthful flair since he's well into his eighties. Never-the-less, his devilish charm intrigued me. Oh, Sheldon, can lightning strike three times? I found Akbar, the love of my life to replace your father, Irving, who at best, was a wonderful provider. Do you think Malcolm was meant to replace Akbar? I wonder.

(She takes a bottle of water from the counter and splashes herself on the chest to cool off.)

SHELDON. *(gives his mother a disgusted look)* For chris-sake, Woman! Have you no shame? Akbar hasn't even been fully digested by the tiger and you're already hitting on husband number three. On a less disgusting note, you'll never guess who I met on the freight train to West Virginia. Elvis Presley! He's heavier than ever, but he still has it. He sang "Don't Be Cruel" ate a pork chop and disappeared. Taking a hint from all this, Memphis is my next stop. P.S. Do you really think Elvis is still alive?

MRS. LEVINE. Yes, Elvis is still alive but in another dimension, which for some reason you were able to connect with. I'm glad you're meeting interesting people. As for the possibility of my having a third husband, let me remind you that if you and that witch doctor had minded your own damn business I'd still be a married woman today. P.S. Malcolm took me to the Rainbow Room at Rockefeller Center and we danced all night. It was fabulous. The only problem was, he has poor vision and is too vain to wear glasses. Every time he dipped me I hit my head on a table. For the past three days the right side of my head has been swollen like a balloon but it's a small price to pay for good company. Love, Mother.

SHELDON. Dear Mother. I arrived in Memphis this morning and did something strange. I stood on a street corner and began singing like Elvis. My hip gyrations were a real crowd pleaser. Six women fainted and a guy named Bruce threw his jock strap at me.

MRS. LEVINE. Dear Sheldon. My nights are filled with Malcom and my days are filled with talk shows. I never miss Oprah or Ellen. I marvel at the depth and insight they possess, as well as their courage to attack such controversial subjects as "Born again Atheists."

SHELDON. Dear Mother. News of the weird. I now not only sing like Elvis, I also eat like him. For breakfast this morning I had five double bacon cheeseburgers and six orders of fries. What do you think is going on? It's like I'm losing Sheldon Levine.

MRS. LEVINE. I've heard of things like this happening, a great artist such as Elvis possessing the soul of a less gifted person like yourself. My feeling is you've got nothing to lose, so go with it. Malcolm took me ice skating in Central Park. He tried to teach me to do a triple axle. The doctor said my hip should be completely healed in eight weeks.

SHELDON. Mother. As I was singing "Blue Suede Shoes," a small, dark man dressed all in white, stepped out of the crowd and handed me a box. Inside was an old costume that Elvis had worn while playing Vegas. There was still a Snickers bar in the pocket. And guess what? A bite was missing. I bet I could sell it on Ebay for a thousand bucks. But I was hungry, so I ate it.

(EXITS to put on Elvis sunglasses and cape)

MRS. LEVINE. Dear Sheldon. It's obvious the man in white was Akbar, who apparently has made peace with the fact that you killed him. If you see him again, don't tell him about Malcolm. Out of common courtesy, I should handle that myself.

SHELDON. *(ENTERS wearing Elvis sunglasses and cape)* Dear Mama. I now not only eat like Elvis, I'm starting to talk like him.

(in Elvis voice)

Uh-huh, Uh huh, Oh, yeah, Thank you very much. Uh huh.

(normal voice)

Elvis was a great singer, but he had a very limited vocabulary.

(EXITS to put on sideburns and belly form)

MRS. LEVINE. Dear Sheldon. Listen to this. Thanks to Malcolm, I'm going to be on Montel Williams Show. That's right. Me! Doris Levine, from New Rochelle! Malcolm has been giving the producer dance lessons and knowing how much I love talk shows, he had me meet him. Well, for some reason, I was more adorable than usual and the producer thought I'd be the perfect guest for next Monday's show. The topic is "Mothers Whose Hearts Have Been Broken By Their Sons." So help me, Sheldon, I'm going to try my best to take your side.

SHELDON. *(ENTERS. In Elvis voice)* Dear Mama. It feels as though I'm time sharing my body with Elvis. I woke up this morning with long sideburns and a gut that looks like the Good Year Blimp. It now seems as if a giant magnet is pulling me to Graceland. Boy, I hope Elvis left some pies in the fridge. Uh-huh, Uh huh, Oh, yeah, Uh huh.

MRS. LEVINE. Believe it or not, I was an absolute smash on Montel. I was biting, yet sensitive. I was shocking, yet conservative. I was determined, yet unassuming. You know, Sheldon, without sounding like I'm blowing my own horn, I can really bullshit with the best of them. I was truly something for everyone. In fact, I was so good I was immediately signed to be on Oprah. Oh, Sheldon, I love being in the spotlight. Next Tuesday I'm on Jerry Springer. I get to throw a chair.

SHELDON. *(in Elvis voice)* Dear Mama. I've been sneaking into Graceland every night. For dinner I eat a gallon of ice cream and a couple dozen Ding Dongs. Then I go to sleep in Elvis' bedroom. The other night I called Priscilla and begged her to come back to me. She called me a maniac and hung up on me. Boy, she's a tough cookie. And speaking of cookies, I just ate four boxes of Lorna Doones and boy am I thirsty. Love, the "King Of Rock'N'Roll."

(EXITS to remove Elvis costume)

MRS. LEVINE. The next time you talk to Priscilla, please ask her what the hell the deal was between Lisa Marie and Michael Jackson. That one still keeps me awake nights. Life is such a mystery. But it's like I said on The Maury Povich Show the other day, "If everything works out the way we want it to, then where the hell's the excitement?" Sometimes even I'm amazed by how deep I can be. Love, Mom. P.S. Malcolm continues to charm the pants off me.

SHELDON. *(ENTERS upstage left behind platform. He leans through the railing, holding on to them as if they were prison cell bars. He is no longer Elvis.)* Keep your pants on, Mom. I have enough problems. This morning when I woke up in Elvis' bedroom there was a SWAT team pointing their guns at me. I was immediately tossed in the county jail. The good news is that my cell mate is a lawyer. The bad news is he refuses to talk to me without a retainer. Love, your jailbird son.

MRS. LEVINE. Sheldon Levine, County Jail, Memphis, Tennessee. Getting tossed in the slammer may be the best thing that ever happened to you. I had a spiritual awakening in a place of solitude. Maybe this is meant to be yours. Love, Mother. P.S. I'm so excited. Malcolm is moving in with me this week. He's the first man I've met without any flaws.

SHELDON. More bad news. I gave the lawyer a retainer. He used it to bail himself out and I've not heard from him since. Worse than that, my new cell mate is an

Evangelist and to pray for my soul, he wants more money than the lawyer.

MRS. LEVINE. Dear Sheldon. I found Malcolm's flaw. He's a cross dresser.

SHELDON. The bad news just got worse. I was sentenced today. I got twenty years in the State Pen. I never should'a called the judge a dumb fart. Love, Prisoner 3-7-16-

MRS. LEVINE & SHELDON. 29-42-43.

MRS. LEVINE. Sheldon, did you notice that your prison numbers are the exact ones Akbar gave you for the lottery? If I were you I'd keep playing them.

SHELDON. Great idea, Mom. I'm sure whenever I want a lottery ticket all I have to do is pull one out of the Warden's ass. Are you nuts. Goddamn it, I'm in a crap hole penal institution, not the Ritz-Carlton.

MRS. LEVINE. Sweetheart. Thanks to your new predicament, I'm going to on Oprah again. The topic is "Mothers With Criminal Children." Try to catch it.

SHELDON. Before I get television privileges in this joint, I need to hammer out five million license plates. I don't get it. How can you be so blasé about my being locked up in one of the worst places imaginable?

MRS. LEVINE. Dear Sheldon. There's something comforting in knowing where your child is at all times. By the way, your father and Akbar appeared before me last night. They've become very good friends and go bowling together in the here-after. They approved of my relationship with Malcolm and thought he looked absolutely smashing in my pink strapless evening gown. When I told them about your ordeal, Akbar pointed out that even in the slammer you're still better off than ninety percent of the people on this planet.

SHELDON. Dear Mother. Tell Akbar he's still an asshole.

MRS. LEVINE. Akbar was not happy with your message and said "May a building fall on you." Be careful. Even though he's dead, he still has connections.

SHELDON. *(crosses downstage left to lowest platform)* Dear Mother. Thank Akbar for his wonderful curse. Last night Tennessee had a major earthquake. My cell started shaking like crazy and suddenly I found myself standing alone in the outside world on a pile of bricks and debris. The prison was right next to a river and I was able to float all the way to Yazoo City, Mississippi on the Warden's bathroom door. I gotta tell you, if I wasn't there to see it for myself, I never would've believed it.

MRS. LEVINE. Dear Sheldon, my fugitive son. Congratulations on your escape from the clink. It's too bad you didn't get to stay long enough to learn a trade. A lot of ex-cons today are making a nice living in the security business. I would like to drop in on you but...

(sighs)

...without Akbar's guidance my mystical abilities seem to have deserted me. I tried contacting you last night through mental telepathy, but all I got was Shirley MacLaine's answering machine.

SHELDON. *(excited)* Mother!

MRS. LEVINE. *(alarmed)* What?

SHELDON. Guess who's back in my life?

MRS. LEVINE. Who?

*(The parrot is tossed to **SHELDON** from offstage left.)*

SHELDON. My parrot Roberto! When I got to Yazoo City he was waiting for me at the post office. You see Mother, you didn't abandon me and neither did he. Anyway, we will stay here in Yazoo waiting for a sign as to what to do next in my search for Sheldon.

MRS. LEVINE. Sheldon! Now it's your turn to guess what?

SHELDON. What?

MRS. LEVINE. Listen to this piece of fabulous news. Because I've consistently been a fascinating guest, I'm getting my own TV talk show.

SHELDON. No?

MRS. LEVINE. Yes. It's called "Ask Doris Anything."

SHELDON. I love the title.

MRS. LEVINE. Oh, Sheldon, it's hard to believe that all this good fortune can happen to little old Doris Levine from New Rochelle.

SHELDON. Well, I'm not surprised. Take it from me, in all the world there is no one like you Ma. Oh, oh, my goodness. Did you hear what I just said? "There's no one in the world like you Ma." You Ma! It's the sign I've been waiting for. I never called you "Ma" before. Don't you see? You Ma! That's where I need to go next. To Yuma, Arizona to search for whatever it is I'm looking for.

MRS. LEVINE. *(a bit doubtful)* You-Ma? Aren't you stretching it a bit?

SHELDON. Not at all. It's as obvious as the love and admiration I have for you. Yuma is where Sheldon Levine needs to be. That's where my answer is. I'm more than sure of that. Oh, Mother, I'm so excited. There seems to be an aura of success and adventure about us, doesn't there?

MRS. LEVINE. Yes. Yes, Sheldon, there certainly does.

SHELDON. And so my quest for the true Sheldon continues. Au revoir, to you Ma. You-Ma! Oh, I just got a chill.

MRS. LEVINE. Maybe take a sweater.

SHELDON. Ta Ta Ma.

(He blows her a kiss and then EXITS upstage left.)

MRS. LEVINE. *(She blows him back a kiss.)* Ta-ta right back to you, darling. Until I hear further, I will send all my letters and an occasional salami to the Post Office in Yuma.

(To Audience. Memorized)

Imagine, my own talk TV show! Boy, oh boy, oh boy, life is a roller coaster. You go up, you go down. You go back, you go forth. You go fast, you go slow. You never know if you're going to make it back dead or alive. But from this day on, one thing is for sure. When it's all over, I'm going to say, "Holy Shit! What a ride!

(blackout)

End of Act I

ACT II

Scene One

(SET NOTE: Downstage center there is now a small low table between two low back chairs.)

(Country-Western Music plays. Lights up stage left as **SHELDON** *ENTERS on the highest platform wearing jeans, flannel shirt, cowboy hat, cowboy boots and carrying a shovel, as he sings a little square dance tune.)*

SHELDON. OH, SWING YOUR PARTNER ROUND THE BEND/ SHOVE HER IN THE BUTT WITH A FOUNTAIN PEN/ CIRCLE RIGHT AND PROMENADE/ THEY SAY SQUARE DANCERS NEVER GET LAID. YES SIRRIEE!

(Music out. He sits on a cube and begins writing.)

Dear Mother. I'm in Beaumont, Texas and making my way towards Yuma where I know I will find whatever it is I seek. To earn a little money I took a job on a ranch cleaning stables. Cowboy life is not as glamorous as it is in the movies. You can't smell horse shit on the big screen. I hope to have enough money to leave Beaumont in a few days. Love, Tex Levine. P.S. My parrot Roberto took off again. When I told him we were on our way to Yuma he mooned me and started flying north. Commitment does not seem to be his strong suit. Oh, well, back to shoveling. DOSEY-DOE AND HOWDY-DOO/ HOW DO YA' GET HORSE PUCKEY OFF YOUR SHOE?

*(**MRS. LEVINE** ENTERS stage right and crosses to the low-back chairs at downstage center. She's wearing a bright, colorful suit, scarf and large framed red glasses. She sits and writes.)*

MRS. LEVINE. Sheldon Levine, General Delivery, Yuma, Arizona. Dear Sheldon. "Ask Doris Anything" is a sensational hit. Everyone is kissing my ass. It feels wonderful. It is so uplifting to have the opportunity to share my gifts of wisdom and gentle-handed guidance with those in need. Incidentally, my first topic was "Children Who Shorten Your Life," but I swear it had nothing to do with you.

SHELDON. *(holds a photograph)* Dear Mother. I'm in a little Texas town called Crockett where I stopped into a thrift shop to buy some pajamas and I discovered a picture of a guy that looked just like Dad with some bimbo on his lap. Had Dad ever been to Texas?

(hands her picture)

MRS. LEVINE. *(looks at picture and then shoves it under her butt and grinds on it in disgust)* Dear Sheldon. I always knew that son-of-a-bitch father of yours was cheating on me. There was no reason why a man who owned one lousy shoe store had to go to as many conventions as he did. Well, he's had it! Tomorrow I'm going to the vault where I stored my fur coats and his ashes and I'm sending him to his no good sister in Miami. Let her take care of that low-life from now on. I know these words of mine might shock you, my being a spiritual person as I am now, as well as a successful talk show host, but every now and then everyone has a karmic set back. Anyway, my subject on today's show will be "Forgiveness – Is it for Everyone?" At this point I don't think so.

SHELDON. Dear Mother. Today I stopped in this Texas town called Irving and I was shocked. Just about everyone there looks like Dad. I also visited an Indian Reservation where there's forty kids and a totem pole that look like Dad too. And here's the freaky thing. The entire town is in the shoe business. It's too bad I didn't get here last week. They had their annual Irving Blowout Sale. Two pairs for the price of one. Didn't Dad used to do that?

MRS. LEVINE. I didn't send your father's remains to his sister. After your last letter I contacted a company in Greenland and arranged to have his ashes dumped as far north as possible. With any luck, right this minute a polar bear is taking a dump on his face. On a brighter note, I can't believe how fascinating my life has become. I'm invited to tons of parties, mingle with world leaders and best of all, the girls in my bridge club are eating their hearts out. I love it. P.S. Last night Malcolm won a beauty contest wearing one of my low cut evening gowns. It only proves when you're hot, you're hot. By the way, Bagel Heaven named a sandwich after me – hot tongue on rye.

SHELDON. Dear Mother. I'm now on a bus loaded with accordion players heading for a polka convention in Waco. What a happy bunch, to be able to find joy and happiness with such awful music.

MRS. LEVINE. Guess what? I made the list of the fifty most exciting people of the year. I was tied for 23rd with none other than your ex-wife, Brenda. What a coincidence. The two most important women in your life still running neck and neck. She looked lovely. How you could let her walk out of your life is a mystery to me.

SHELDON. Dear Mom. I got off the polka bus. After five hours of seeing the same scenery over and over I realized the driver was stuck in a traffic circle.

MRS. LEVINE. Dear Sheldon. There's something safe about going nowhere. Here I am on the fast track and it's absolutely exhausting me. And the tabloids are so vicious. Yesterday the Inquirer ran a story about me having an affair with Jack Nicholson. Of course it's not true, but that didn't stop Malcom from going into a jealous rage. He chopped the heels off all my Jimmy Choos.

SHELDON. I'm in New Mexico now. I was invited to share a teepee with a guy who was either a Hopi or a hippie. I wasn't sure. He gave me something to smoke and I was out for three days. It gave me time to think. Mostly about you and the sincere and caring person you've become. I wonder if there has ever been a Saint from New Rochelle. If not, I'd like to put you up for nomination. Saint Doris. Saint Doris Levine. Yes, I like that.

MRS. LEVINE. Dear Sheldon. Being a TV star isn't as easy as it looks. There were four fist fights on my show last week. I started three of them. I'm sure even Gandhi would want to take a swing at some of these nut jobs.

SHELDON. Dear Mother. For the first time in my life I've begun to see the world around me. Just this morning I watched a humming bird suck nectar from a flower. It was beautiful to see nature nurturing nature. Oh, Mother, I want to fill the whole world with love, just like I know you do. Right now I'm going to hug a cactus.

MRS. LEVINE. Sheldon, I urge you not to get too in touch with yourself. I'm starting to discover that the more awareness one has, the more unfairness one sees. And it's always the same thing over and over. "Doris it's not my fault! Doris it's not my fault!" Well, one thing's for sure, it's not my fault.

SHELDON. I just came back from spending two days in the hospital. As I was hugging a cactus, a rattlesnake came along and bit me in the ass. It seems that's what rattlesnakes do so I'm trying not to take it personally. Painfully yours, Sheldon.

MRS. LEVINE. Dear Sheldon. Serenity and decency are proving to be very lonely qualities. All I deal with are wimps and losers. So help me Sheldon, some days I feel like telling them all to blow it out their butts. I wouldn't be surprised if every talk show host feels the same way. No wonder Rosie quit "The View."

SHELDON. Oh, Mother! This morning I danced on the rim of the Grand Canyon naked. To have the wind blow between my loins was magical. I got frostbite on my left nut, but it was worth it. I should be in Yuma in a few days. I can't wait to pick up your spiritually uplifting letters.

MRS. LEVINE. Dear Sheldon. "Ask Doris Anything" is really starting to get on my nerves. The whole world's coming to me with their problems, but who the hell gives a damn about my problems? And don't think I don't have any. A dead first husband who populated half the state of Texas. A dead second husband who hardly visits anymore and a boyfriend who looks better in my clothes than I do. I'll be honest, Sheldon, my only source of strength seems to be in my renewed interest in red meat.

SHELDON. Dear Mother. I've written my first chant. It really calms my soul. OOOMA OOOMA OOOMA/I'M ON MY WAY TO YUMA/IN YUMA I WILL BLOOMA/ OOOMA OOOMA OOOMA

MRS. LEVINE. *(takes off glasses and scarf and tosses them in the kitchen trash can)* I quit my show. A person can take just so much bullshit. People got problems, screw 'em. Let them work it out for themselves. That's what I have to do. As for your chant, it reminds me of your poetry. Need I say more?

SHELDON. Dear Mother. I'm forty miles outside of Yuma where I hope to attain the same love and concern for mankind that you have embraced.
OOMA, OOMA, OOMA
I HOPE I DON'T MEET A PUMA.

MRS. LEVINE. Sheldon, it's really bugging me that while I'm getting your letters, all my letters are collecting dust in a Yuma Post Office. Anyway, I rejoined my bridge club again. The gossip and back-stabbing was even more invigorating than I remembered. I took Malcolm with me. Mrs. Krinski couldn't take her eyes off of him. It's eating her up that men are still attracted to me and she can't get squat. Well, ha ha to her.

SHELDON. Dear Mother. In homage to my admiration for you, I've decided to make the rest of the pilgrimage on my knees.

(He drops to his knees and moves a few inches forward.)
OOMA, OOMA, OOMA.

MRS. LEVINE. Oooma oooma oooma my ass. Get off your knees. All you're doing is putting holes in your pants. Now listen to this horror story. Mrs. Krinski kidnapped my Malcolm. That's right! That bitch ran off with him. I keep telling myself I'm better off without him, but he took three of my best dresses. Let me tell you this now, Sheldon, so you can't say I didn't warn you. Basically, the world is shit. Either you hold your breath until you die, so you don't smell it, or you learn to be shit too. I'm leaning towards the latter. Love, Mother.

SHELDON. Thanks to the oppressive heat, the clarity of my journey has become even more evident. I now realize that compassion is what I've been searching for. It's what you have in your heart and now I have it too. Oh, Mom. I feel a stronger bond than ever between you and me and all God's creatures

(slaps a mosquito on his neck)

Except maybe mosquitoes. That one I don't get.

MRS. LEVINE. I found out that tramp Mrs. Krinski is taking my Malcolm to Hawaii on a honeymoon. With an ass as big as hers, the whole island will be under water in minutes. I've never hated so many people as I do now, which incidentally is not a bad thing since, chances are they deserve it, and frankly, it makes me feel better.

SHELDON. *(exalted)* Yuma! Yuma at last. Oh, Mom, this journey has opened a window to my soul. I can't wait to read all your letters of hope and joy that await me. Unfortunately, I have not been able to find anyone who knows where the post office is. But I'll keep asking. By the way, I've taken the name Kashusha. I feel it is much more poetic than Sheldon. Love, Kashusha.

MRS. LEVINE. Dear Kashusha. Is this what a mother raises a son for? To change his name to Kashusha? To make a goddamn fool out of himself? Grow up, Kashusha. This is not the sixties anymore. When I see the pleasure that Mrs. Katz gets from her son, Larry, the chiropractor, I realize how short changed I was by you. Anyway, once again it's Mother's Day and once again I'm spending it disappointed. Don't take this the wrong way, Sheldon, but like everything else in my life, Mother's Day just never lived up to my expectations.

(She EXITS Stage right to put on the housecoat and slippers she wore in Act I, Scene 1.)

SHELDON. Mom. I just passed a drug store and lo and behold, what did I see but a big sign that said "Remember Mom on Her Day." Well, tears came to my eyes. Not just because I didn't have any money to buy you a card, but because this is the first Mother's Day I can honestly and wholeheartedly celebrate the true meaning of the word "Mother." So I've written you my own card and it comes straight from my heart. Dear Mom. ROSES ARE RED/ VIOLETS ARE BLUE/ JUST CALL ME MR. LUCKY/ CAUSE I GOT A MOM LIKE YOU. Love, Kashusha.

MRS. LEVINE. Dear Mr. Lucky Kashusha. Thanks for your mercifully short poem. I still find it lacking in substance, but then the last thing anyone should be is a critic. Now here's something important you can dwell on. For Mother's Day, Mrs. Minkus's son bought her a new car. Since she can't drive, she going to use it as an extra room to play mah jong in. Learn from this Sheldon. That's what I call a son and that's what I call a gift. When I think of some of the gifts you gave me for Mother's Day, I could puke.

*(A shocked **SHELDON** ENTERS upstage left with a pile of letters tied in a bundle with string.)*

SHELDON. Mother! I picked up all the mail you sent me since I escaped from prison. Oh, my God, what the hell happened? You've gone back to being the same angry wacko you always were. To even think that we could finally have a meaningful relationship was a pointless waste because nothing I do will ever be enough for you. Well, I'm not letting you make me nuts again. I'm through with pain. Goodbye forever you…you…you LUNATIC!

(He EXITS upstage left.)

MRS. LEVINE. Lunatic! Lunatic!

(She takes a deep breath. Her anger builds.)

Well, Sheldon, maybe I am a lunatic. Maybe you have to be in order to survive in today's world. How sane do you really want to be knowing we live in a world where the ice caps are melting, the ozone layer is disintegrating, and the bees are dropping like flies. We're forced to live with dirty air, acid rain and undrinkable water. Doesn't it bother you, my dear son, that the meat they sell us is so full of steroids, the cows could play basketball for the Knicks? Does it burn your ass, Sheldon, as it does mine, that those sleazeball politicians we elect to take care of us all have better retirement and medical plans than we do? And all this new technology that's supposed to make life better doesn't do anything except give me a headache. Download, upload, Blackberry, blueberry, cell phones, iPods, Google, Yahoo, My Space, outer space, tweeter, peter and that W-W-W-Dot Com Shit! Just how good is that for one's mental well being? Huh? Huh? And everywhere you go, people giving you the finger. My landlord, my paper boy and that nun I sometimes sit next to on the bus… You want to know why? Because the world is full of people wound so tight that any minute they can snap like a pretzel. Sanity, Sheldon? Why? What's the point? Let me tell you kiddo, if one morning you wake up and you're not a lunatic, there's something seriously wrong with you.

(a beat)

Dear Sheldon. It's been weeks since I've heard from you. Was it something I said?

(a beat)

It's been several months and still no word from you. Even the mailman is starting to ask questions.

(a beat)

MRS. LEVINE. *(cont.)* Sheldon Levine. Department of Missing Persons, United States of America. Dear Sheldon. My last letter sent to Yuma was returned to me. I've gone to the police but they're so busy trying to stay out of jail themselves that until you're missing for at least five years they don't want to be bothered. So I'm taking matters into my own hands. I'm putting your picture on a milk carton. I'm paying extra for chocolate.

(A beat. She crosses to downstage center to the chairs and sits.)

Dear Sheldon. It's now been six months since I've heard from you so if you decide to come home and if I'm not here, check the hospitals. If I'm not there, check the cemeteries.

(SHELDON ENTERS upstage left on the top platform wearing a minstrel's hat and carrying a ukulele. He strums a chord and begins singing to the melody of GREENSLEEVES.)

SHELDON.
> ALAS MY MOM, YOU HAVE DONE ME WRONG
> TO DRIVE ME NUTS MY WHOLE LIFE LONG
> YOU PUT ME THROUGH PAIN,
> YOU DROVE ME TO TEARS
> YOU BUSTED MY BALLS FOR THIRTY SOME YEARS

MRS. LEVINE. It's been a whole year since I've heard from you. Mrs. Krinski passed away and no one can find Malcolm or my dresses. It seems the world has all but forgotten me. Certainly my son has. Sometimes I think the only reason for having children is so that when death comes you won't mind it so much.

SHELDON. *(strumming a chord)*
> YOUR NAGGING AND BITCHING IS INFINITE
> YOU'VE TURNED MY LIFE INTO TOTAL SHIT
> I TRIED TO BE GOOD, I TRIED TO BE KIND
> BUT YOU DROVE ME OUT OF MY GODDAMN MIND

MRS. LEVINE. It's been eighteen months and still no word from you. Are you dead? If so, send a sign. I heard Houdini was able to talk to his mother after he died. But then I guess he cared about her. By the way, your parrot Roberto came back. I opened the window to shake out some crumbs from the tablecloth and he just flew in. He seems content here and while we don't really speak to one another, there seems to be a mutual respect. If only I could have worked out something like that with you.

SHELDON. *(strums chord)*
DORIS LEVINE, THE GUILT TRIP QUEEN
YOU'VE CARRIED INSANITY TO THE EXTREME
BUT SOMEHOW I'LL SALVAGE MY SELF ESTEEM
JUST WAIT, DEAR DORIS LEVINE,
JUST WAIT, DEAR DORIS LEVINE,
JUST WAIT, DEAR DORIS LEVINE

(He EXITS upstage left.)

MRS. LEVINE. Dear Sheldon. It's been two and a half years since I last heard from you and frankly I hardly ever think about you anymore. I stopped playing bridge with the girls because I'm sick and tired of them bragging about how much happiness their kids have brought them. Besides I can't bear to look at one more photo album of their cute little grandchildren at Disney World. I would have liked to have had grandchildren, Sheldon. It's really too bad you couldn't have straightened things out with Brenda. You two would have had very pretty children. Sure, most likely the would have needed their noses fixed, but I would have gladly come up with the money.

(A beat. She has mellowed.)

Dear Sheldon. Well, now it's over five years that I haven't heard from you. Have I lost you forever? If that's the case, my goodness, wouldn't that be a final kick in the ass for Doris Levine, a mother who's only sin was loving her son too much. I will admit that at times I was a bit overbearing, but I always tried to be overbearing in a very positive way. I'll tell you, Sheldon, motherhood is the most misunderstood occupation in the world. I started to think about forgiveness again. I know I told you it wasn't for everyone and I still feel that's true. But I think that sometimes we confuse forgiveness with letting go. There is a big difference. Forgiveness is for those you truly want back in your life. Letting go is for those you don't want back. I want you back in my life, Sheldon. So if by chance it's you who has to forgive me, then you should seriously consider it, because I've forgiven you. I miss you, Sheldon. I think I've mellowed. I never thought that it was possible to love someone to death. But maybe I have.

(sighs)

(Sound: Doorbell)

MRS. LEVINE. *(cont.)* Come in! The door's open. It's always open.

(SHELDON ENTERS *stage right. He is nicely dressed in a suit and tie.* **MRS. LEVINE** *looks at him and rises as he slowly comes to her. The following should be performed memorized and staged.)*

Sheldon?

SHELDON. Hi, Mom.

MRS. LEVINE. It's really you? You're not dead?

SHELDON. No, I'm not dead. I'm more alive than I've ever been. And guess what? My answer was in Yuma after all.

MRS. LEVINE. No kidding?

SHELDON. You see, after I read all your letters, I had a nervous breakdown.

MRS. LEVINE. So that's why you didn't write to me. I feel so much better.

SHELDON. Well, while being strapped down, heavily medicated and getting daily high-intensity shock treatments, I watched as these incredible servants of science were able to mend my broken spirit and breathe life into my tormented soul.

MRS. LEVINE. *(softly, fearful)* You're not still writing poetry?

SHELDON. No.

MRS. LEVINE. *(relieved)* Good.

SHELDON. I was in complete awe of these therapeutic guardians of sanity. The power they had to get inside my mind and re-arrange it. They were so confident, so skillful, so well dressed. And I began to think, if I admired someone like this, why wouldn't you?

MRS. LEVINE. Of course. That goes without saying.

SHELDON. *(removes a scroll of paper from his vest pocket. He hands it to her.)* Here! This will explain everything.

MRS. LEVINE. *(reading)* Awarded to Sheldon Levine from the University of Yuma...Oh, my God, Sheldon. You're a...

(puzzled)

You're a therapist?

SHELDON. Yes, I'm a *therapist*. I'm self-assured, I stand up straighter, I have nice office furniture and most of all I'm someone of significance. And I realize that this is what you wanted for me all along.

MRS. LEVINE. A therapist with nice office furniture. It's every mother's dream.

SHELDON. *(pointing to diploma)* I have a Masters Degree *and* a P-h-D.

MRS. LEVINE. *(delighted)* A P-h-D? Then you're a doctor too?

*(***SHELDON*** nods.)*

A doctor. Wait till I tell the girls. This will eat them up alive.

SHELDON. Then I've finally made you happy?

MRS. LEVINE. *(She strokes his face.)* Absolutely. It just goes to show you Sheldon, that all the anguish, all the grief, all the suffering...

SHELDON. That you put me through.

MRS. LEVINE. *(nodding, with a bit of guilt)* Yes.

SHELDON. It was all worth it and I forgive you.

(He kisses her forehead.)

MRS. LEVINE. Forgiveness! How do you like that. I knew I was on to something.

SHELDON. *(He flashes a dark smile at the audience. He then leads her downstage left to the lowest platform.)* And now that I'm on solid mental ground, I'm going to dedicate my life to making others just as healthy as I am.

MRS. LEVINE. And to think, I'm responsible for that. Oh, Sheldon, someday, you will have children who will need the same delicate care and guidance that you had.

(She lies down on the lowest platform, ready for analysis. He sits near her head.)

SHELDON. I hear what you're saying. Go on.

(He takes out a small pad and pen from his jacket, prepared to write down notes as she speaks.)

MRS. LEVINE. Remember all the nice things I did for you? Like how I insisted on riding on the school bus with you every day and how I potty trained you at the duck pond in Central Park. And all the problems I had breast feeding you in public. The way people stared.

SHELDON. *(refreshing her memory)* I was six years old.

MRS. LEVINE. Oh, Sheldon, isn't it wonderful that you and I have been given a second chance?

SHELDON. Yes. Yes it is.

(clears his throat)

Now let's talk about your childhood, shall we Doris?

MRS. LEVINE. Well, my mother and I were very different. She was an extremely difficult woman.

*(**SHELDON** nods as he continues to take notes.)*

SHELDON. Really?

MRS. LEVINE. You have no idea. Controlling like you wouldn't believe. Manipulative, conniving...

(The stage begins to darken.)

SHELDON. Go on.

MRS. LEVINE. Nosy, bitter.

(sitting up)

Oh, Sheldon, you are so lucky you didn't have her for a mother.

*(**SHELDON** nods as he continues to take notes.)*

(slow fade to black)

(curtain)

COSTUMES

Act I – Scene 1
MRS. LEVINE: Housecoat, slippers
SHELDON: Sweatshirt, pants, casual shoes, head bandages (small & large)

Act I – Scene 2
MRS. LEVINE: Sari, sandals and fabric shoulder bag/pouch
SHELDON: Same as Act I, Scene 1

Act I – Scene 3
MRS. LEVINE: Black suit, blouse, shoes
SHELDON: Light jacket over same sweatshirt, pants, casual shoes. Elvis sunglasses, white sequined cape, side burns, belly form

Act II – Scene 1
MRS. LEVINE: Colorful pant suit, scarf, large framed glasses, high heels. Same housecoat and slippers as in Act I, Scene 1
SHELDON: Jeans, flannel shirt, cowboy hat, cowboy boots.
Minstrel's hat, suit, shirt, tie, dress shoes

PROPS

Stack of junk mail
5 journals (Mrs. Levine: 3 for Act I, 1 for Act II; Sheldon: 1 for entire play)
Pens
Pastry
Enormous juvenile birthday card
Letter to Sheldon from Mrs. Levine (left on kitchen counter)
Prop Parrot
Letter to Mrs. Levine from Sheldon (left on kitchen counter)
Small Backpack
Small bottle of water
Shovel
Photograph
Bundle of letters tied with string
Ukulele
Diploma – rolled and tied with ribbon
Small note book and pen for Sheldon

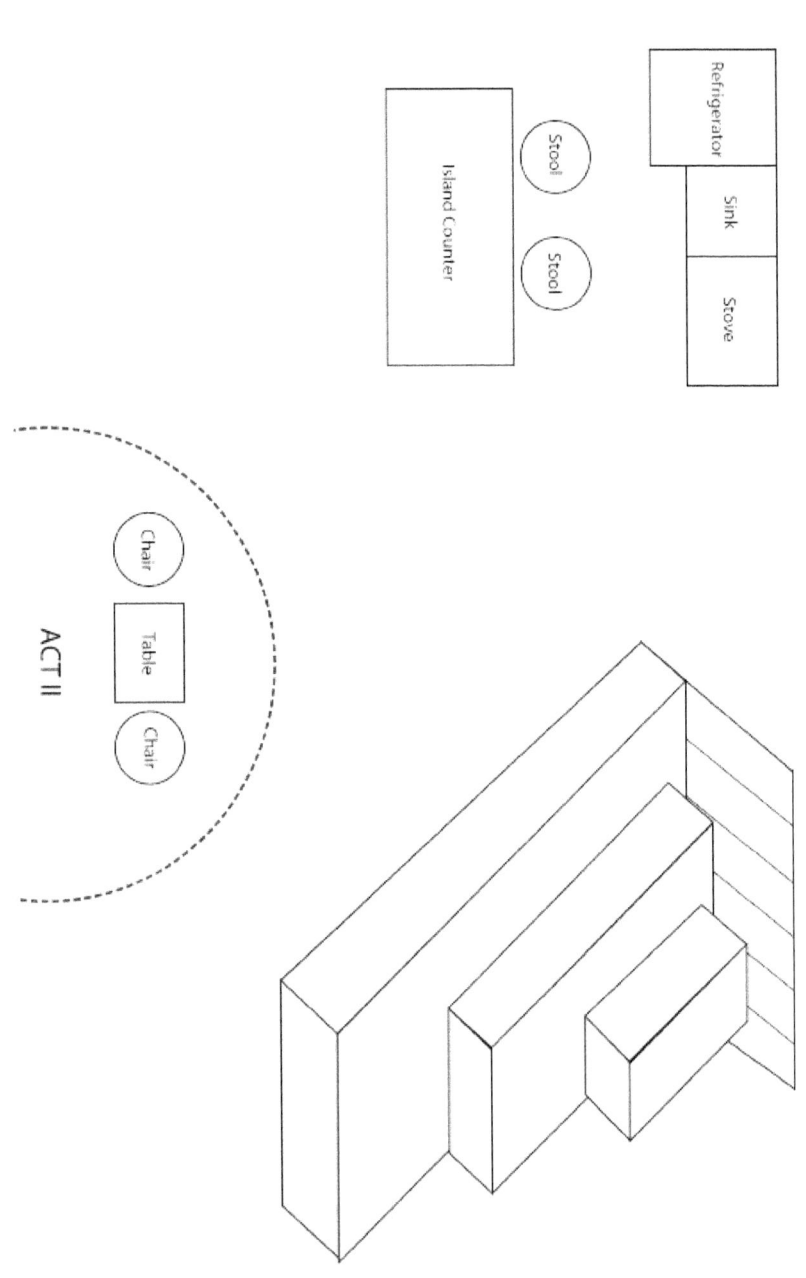

From the Reviews of
THE OUTRAGEOUS ADVENTURES OF SHELDON & MRS. LEVINE...

"Side-splitting, off the wall surprises."
– Nathalie Plotkin, *Montery County Herald*

"A laugh a minute good time farce."
– Pat Taylor, *The Tolucan Times*

"Plenty of big laughs…as both characters spiral toward insanity."
– Pauline Ademek, *Studio City Sun*

www.ingramcontent.com/pod-product-compliance
Lightning Source LLC
Chambersburg PA
CBHW070650300426
44111CB00013B/2361